The Fat Counter

Jane Thomas obtained a BSc in Nutrition at London University in 1971 and went on to Montreal where she obtained her postgraduate qualification in dietetics. Following completion of a Master of Medical Science degree, she joined the Health Education Council in 1974 and was their Research Officer until 1979 when she took up the post of Lecturer in Social Nutrition at Queen Elizabeth College, University of London. In addition to writing and broadcasting on the subject of healthy eating, her other activities include bringing up her two young children in Oxford where she lives with her dentist husband.

Jane Thomas
with a foreword by
Dr Alan Maryon-Davis

The Fat Counter

Pan Original
Pan Books London and Sydney

First published 1985 by Pan Books Ltd,
Cavaye Place, London SW10 9PG
9 8 7 6 5 4 3 2 1

ISBN 0 330 28775 3
Photoset by Parker Typesetting Service, Leicester
Printed in Great Britain by
Richard Clay (The Chaucer Press) Ltd,
Bungay, Suffolk

Contents

Acknowledgements

In the case of most unbranded foods, the figures given are taken from McCance and Widdowsons's *The Composition of Foods* (4th edition) by A. A. Paul and D. A. T. Southgate, 1978, HMSO. Where British figures are not available, American data has been used in some cases, from the US Department of Agriculture handbook.

In addition grateful thanks are due to the many people, nutritionists, food scientists, analysts and quality control managers who provided details of the fat content of manufactured foods.

Foreword

Dr Alan Maryon-Davis MB BChir MSc MRCP MFCM
Chief Medical Officer to the Health Education Council

Over the past few years there has been so much conflicting advice about healthy eating and dieting that you could be forgiven for thinking that it's all far too confusing, that the diet experts can't even agree amongst themselves, and that you might as well stop worrying about it and eat what you like, when you like and as much as you like.

Unfortunately, by doing that you could be making the biggest mistake of your life . . . literally.

There is now very clear scientific evidence that the sort of diet most people are eating in modern industrialized nations like ours is a major cause of ill-health. Heart disease, the single biggest killer in the Western world, is closely linked to dietary factors; especially the amount of fatty foods we eat. So too is high blood pressure (hypertension) and severe overweight (obesity), both of which can lead to a number of serious disorders. And many cases of cancer –perhaps as many as one in three – are thought to be linked to our high fat/low fibre diet.

A number of major reports, recently published, have carefully sifted all the evidence concerning the way our food can affect our health, and all of them agree on the basic principles of healthy eating. One of the clear messages to emerge is that we should make a determined effort to eat less fat – especially so-called saturated fat, which comes mainly from dairy products and meat, and makes up the bulk of the fat in our diet. The UK Department of Health's recommendation is that we should cut saturated fat by a quarter, starting right now, in order to reduce our risk – and more particularly our children's risk – of suffering from heart disease and related disorders in years to come.

But if we are to cut the fat in our food we need to know where it is. Although much of it is obvious enough – butter, margarine, cooking fats and oils, cream, the fat on meat – an awful lot is 'hidden' in processed foods, made-up meals, sausages, hamburgers, cheeses, chocolate and all manner of foods that you would never think of as fatty.

The trouble is that there's no easy way of finding out exactly how much fat there is in the food you are eating. The obvious place to put that sort of information is on the label or packet. And yet, despite strong pressure from consumers, nutritionists and doctors to label foods with their fat content, particularly their saturated fat content, it looks as though it is going to be quite a while before the food industry responds.

That is why Jane Thomas has compiled this book. Here you will find the facts about fat and health clearly explained. Here you will find down-to-earth practical advice on choosing, shopping for and cooking lower fat meals. And here you will find the fat content of hundreds of food items, painstakingly compiled in one of the most comprehensive lists available.

I heartily recommend this little book. It has just the information you need as you go round the supermarket, and I'm quite sure you'll find it an invaluable guide to a healthier and slimmer future . . . for you and your family.

Alan Maryon-Davis

Introduction

Fat makes food palatable and we naturally buy the tastiest food we can afford. So it's hardly surprising that when people have more money to spend on food the pattern all over the world seems to be the same. They eat more fat. After all we talk about successful people living off 'the fat of the land' – not the protein or carbohydrate.

Back in 1863 a dietary survey by Dr Edward Smith showed that the ordinary working man in Britain was eating about 55 grams of fat each day. Today that figure has risen to 104 grams. Quite a change – and in recent years scientific evidence has been mounting up which suggests that all this fat is not doing our health much good. But you can only spread so much on a piece of bread, so where is all this fat coming from? When people become more affluent they like to buy larger quantities of foods they enjoy, like meat, cheese and dairy products rather than filling up on cheaper low-fat foods like bread and potatoes. That's where the trouble starts. But another major difference from a century ago is the extent to which we rely on processed foods. About three-quarters of our food has been processed in some way and the techniques used may well involve the addition of fat. We may add further fat ourselves when we choose frying as a quick cooking method. The changing pace of life has resulted in the appearance of the 'fast-food' market, the takeaway, and an increasing emphasis on convenience. In a recent survey, two-thirds of the people questioned had eaten take-away food in the last month. And it's not just a matter of a quick meal at a counter or the office desk – the same survey showed that 80% of take-away food is actually eaten in the home. Although 'fast food' tends to conjure up an image of slick service and hamburgers, this £1000 million market also includes pizza, ethnic takeaways and fried chicken, as well as the traditional fish and chips. Which all adds up to something in the region of 18,500 outlets offering food with the emphasis on convenience and usually a pretty high fat content.

So we tend to eat more fat, not only as 'visible' fats like butter, margarine, the fat on meat, cooking fat and oils, but also 'invisible' fats in milk, cheese, nuts, lean meats, meat products and a host of other foods. But all fat has one thing in common, wherever you find it – it is a concentrated source of energy. A gram of fat will give you nine calories, more than twice as many as the same weight of protein or carbohydrate. This is very useful if you are a lumberjack or work at the coalface. By including plenty of fat in your diet it is possible to get all the energy you need without wading through vast quantities of stodgy food, which most of us would find quite daunting. However, for the semi-sedentary majority, there is quite a different problem – because it tastes so nice, it is easy to eat large amounts of high-fat food which will provide lots of calories that we don't really need.

Perhaps it's not surprising then that surveys suggest that about one third of Britain's adult population is overweight. A recent report on obesity from the Royal College of Physicians recognized the contribution to this problem made by excess fat intake, resulting in a range of recommendations. They suggested that cookery instruction in schools should emphasize meals with a lower fat content and that meals provided by institutions – hospitals schools, canteens, etc. – should contain less fat than at present. Even more importantly, they called on the agricultural industry, food manufacturers, and government departments to cooperate in ensuring that the food products available have a lower fat content, which the consumer should be aware of through better labelling. At the present time it is very hard to judge how much fat is in the foods we eat.

And that is why this book has been compiled – so that you can find out the fat content of different foods and decide what changes you can make to cut down the amount of fat you eat. But why should you want to make changes? One reason, which has been mentioned already, may be important for a lot of people – cutting down on calories and looking slim and attractive. But there's more to all this than just looking good. Being overweight is not only a social liability. It also increases the risk of a variety of health problems, especially if you have a family tendency to high blood pressure, diabetes, or heart disease. Just a few extra pounds bodyweight can make all the difference to whether or when you may develop the same problems.

For people who are more seriously overweight, those defined as 'obese' (more than 20% heavier than the desirable weight for their height) the list of potential health hazards is a lengthy one. In addition to diabetes, hypertension and cardiovascular problems there is an increased risk of gall bladder disease. Strain is put on the weight-bearing joints of the body, like the knees, so that arthritis, back trouble and painful feet are common. Varicose veins are more likely to occur, and when it comes to an operation for this, or any other reason, the obese person is at greater risk, partly because all that extra body fat makes breathing difficult. Even under normal circumstances, breathlessness can make any form of exertion unpleasant. Which all adds up to shorter life expectancy in the seriously overweight. This is hardly news; Hippocrates in 400BC wrote that 'fat men are more likely to die suddenly than the slender', an observation which has been borne out by modern studies.

But concern about fat in the diet goes far beyond the problem of overweight. A high intake of fat has been linked to other conditions often referred to as the 'diseases of western civilization'. There is increasing evidence linking environmental factors and diet to various forms of cancer, although the exact way in which these are caused is still far from clear. A variety of factors often contribute to these diseases. Heart disease for example, seems linked to diet, smoking and lack of exercise as well as family history. One way scientists use to separate the effect of a family tendency towards a particular illness from the effects of lifestyle and the environment, is by looking at the health of groups of people who have migrated from one country to another. Their genes remain the same, but the environment changes. In the case of cancer, it seems that migrants tend to take on the cancer pattern of the host country. This suggests that lifestyle and environmental factors have a large part to play in the causation of many forms of cancer. One group who have been studied are the Japanese in America; they have rates of cancer which match those of American whites more closely than those of Japanese people living in Japan.

In this country, lung cancer is the most commonly fatal kind, and the environmental factor linked with that is, of course, smoking. But cancer of the large bowel (colon) is the second most frequent killer and seems to be on the increase. Studies of different populations around the world tend to suggest that this form of cancer may be linked to a high-fat diet, especially where the fibre intake is also low. Some research has also found an association between rates of breast cancer and the amount of fat which is usually eaten. Breast cancer seems to be more common amongst groups of people whose diet contains more fat. There is still a lot of research to be done in this field, just as there is in relation to that most contentious of topics – diet and the western epidemic of heart disease.

To call it an 'epidemic' is no exaggeration. In England and Wales each year, there are nearly thirty thousand deaths in men under the age of sixty-five due to coronary heart disease. That is an annual loss of a quarter of a million years of 'working life'. But what has really been causing concern is that in recent years the death rates from heart disease have been going down dramatically in countries like the USA, Canada, New Zealand, Belgium and Finland – but not in the UK. When Scotland, Northern Ireland, and England and Wales were considered separately, they occupied three of the top five positions in a world ranking of death rates from coronary heart disease. For this reason a panel of experts was appointed by the Department of Health to examine carefully the scientific evidence on diet and heart disease, and to come up with some recommendations. Since the 1950s, a large question mark has hung over fat as one of the possible culprits. Worldwide studies have shown a striking link between heart disease and the amount of fat in the diet. And the strongest link seems to be with a particular kind of fat – saturated fat. Studies of different populations throughout the world show that the proportion of saturated fat in the diet is closely correlated to the death rate from heart disease. Experiments have shown that eating food which contains a lot of saturated fat tends to push up the level of fatty substances in the blood (blood cholesterol). This seems to happen to a greater extent in some people than in others, depending on their genes. And people with a high blood cholesterol level are more likely to have a heart attack or angina, particularly if they have a family history of heart disease.

So it is hardly surprising that the most important recommendation for the public in the experts' report, published by the UK Department of Health in 1984, concerns the amount and type of fat we eat. After considering all the available information, they advise that the average person should cut back on the total amount of fat they eat by one-sixth and reduce the amount of saturated fat by about a quarter. The experts recommend that people should aim to get about 35% of their food energy from fat and that less than half of this (15%) should be in the form of saturated fat.

How can this advice be put into practice? And what is a saturated fat? When we talk about the fat content of a food, as in this book, we refer to the total amount of fatty substances present (that is triglycerides, phospholipids and sterols). In order to cut down the total fat then, it is best to choose from those foods that have a lower fat content and to follow up the practical suggestions in the section on page 68. When it comes to saturated fat perhaps a little more detail may be helpful. Chemically, food fats consist mainly of mixtures of triglycerides. Each triglyceride is made up of three units called fatty acids. And the differences between one fat or oil and another largely depend on the particular combination of fatty acids in the triglycerides. These fatty acids can either be 'saturated' or 'unsaturated'. So that when people talk of a food being 'high in saturated fat' it means that most of the fatty acid units making up the triglycerides are of the saturated kind. A fat 'high in polyunsaturates' would be made up of triglycerides where more of the fatty acids were of the unsaturated kind.

If you are still trying to visualize a saturated or unsaturated fatty acid a rather bizarre metaphor may help. Imagine some hedgehogs and a box of polystyrene balls. If a hedgehog rolled in the box, lots of balls would stick on its spines. A saturated fatty acid is a like a hedgehog with polystyrene balls on every one of its spines. An unsaturated fatty acid is like a hedgehog who still has some spines without balls on (the more free spines, the more unsaturated). Now these hedgehogs always travel in threes (triglycerides). And the final appearance of the troop of hedgehogs (fat or oil) will depend on whether you have more hedgehogs completely covered in balls, or more with only a few polystyrene balls stuck on their spines.

Some fats, such as lard or butter, are quite solid at room temperature, and these have a high level of saturated fat. Oils are really only fats that are liquid at room temperature, usually as a result of having a higher content of unsaturated fatty acids. Margarine is made by taking oils and adding hydrogen to those unsaturated fatty acids to make them saturated, and the product hard. (The poor old unsaturated hedgehog is dropped back in the box again to make sure it gets balls stuck on all its spines.) This is the reason why margarine may not necessarily be any healthier for you than butter. Hard margarines may contain just as much saturated fat. It all depends on the brand and the extent of this 'hydrogenation'. A soft margarine is more likely to contain higher levels of polyunsaturates.

Let's put this complicated picture in practical perspective. The more saturated fats usually come from animal sources, meat, dairy products, and most margarines. Whereas the less saturated fats are found mostly in vegetable oils. But there are some important exceptions to this simple rule. Chicken, turkey, rabbit, and oily fish like herring have fats which are less saturated than other animal fats. And two plant oils, coconut and palm oil, are highly saturated. So when choosing fats for a healthier diet its best to cut down overall and try to choose from the right hand side of the following table rather than the left.

Foods containing mainly saturated fats	*Foods containing mainly unsaturated fats*
Beef, pork, mutton	Maize oil i.e. corn oil
Butter, most margarine, lard	Sunflower oil
Cooking fats	Safflower oil
Coconut oil	Soya bean oil
Palm oil	Most nuts (except cashews and coconut)
Milk	Fish
Cheese	Fish oils
	Fish liver oils (cod, halibut)
	Chicken and turkey

This book will help you to find out just where the fat in your diet is coming from and enable you to reduce it by choosing lower fat alternatives. In a healthier diet with less fat more of the calories should come from starchy foods like fruit and vegetables. The section of this book on low fat cooking and eating gives some practical hints.

With all this talk about fats and health, it's tempting to think that it might be best to avoid fat altogether. But apart from the fact that most people would find it very unpleasant, not to say impossible, to eliminate all fat from their diet, it would also be inadvisable from a nutritional point of view. Some important vitamins come to us dissolved in the fats and oils we eat. Vitamins A, D, E and K do not dissolve in water as other vitamins do. So if we eliminated fat altogether we would be short of these. In addition, a dietary source of linoleic acid, an unsaturated fatty acid, is essential because the body cannot make its own supply. So there are some very important nutritional benefits from the fat in the foods we eat. With the help of this book you should be able to adjust the quantity you eat so that these benefits are not outweighed by the hazards of eating too much fat.

What the figures mean

The food listings which follow give the fat content (either as grams per 100 grams or grams per ounce) of many common foods. But the first point that anyone using these tables must bear in mind is that very few foods have a constant composition. For example, there may be seasonal changes. An extreme case of this is the avocado, where the fat content can range from 11 to 39g/100g. On the other hand, manufactured products are usually the subject of quality control and may, therefore, have a much more constant composition. However, from time to time food manufacturers may alter the recipe or process they use which will affect the fat content. This may result in some variation from the figures given in the listing as supplied at the time of going to press. The figures listed give the average fat content of the food as it is eaten – that is excluding bones, shells, etc.

Cooking methods can also affect the fat content of a food item and, where appropriate, different methods of preparing the same food have been included. The amount of fat in home-cooked dishes will depend on the recipe you use. But a number of popular dishes have been included and the figures given are based on typical recipes. When it comes to making up dried products, once again the final fat content can vary. Listings are given either by dry weight or for the product made up as per the manufacturers' instructions. The fat per 100g or ounce will naturally be lower once the water has been added. So if you are making comparisons, be sure that you are comparing like with like (not *regular* mashed potato with *dry* 'instant' potato, for example).

Most fruits and vegetables contain only traces of fat. Those which appear in the tables either naturally contain a measurable amount or are usually prepared in such a way as to increase the fat content. Similarly alcoholic beverages and carbonated drinks are fat-free and have therefore been excluded. The only exception to this is advocaat which has been listed.

Abbreviations and some conversion factors

Tr = trace
0 = nil
1 gram (g) = 1,000 milligrams (mg)
1 ounce (oz) = 28g
100g = 3½ oz

Food Listings

Product	Brand/comments	Fat (g/100g)	Fat (g/oz)
Ackee (canned)		15.2	4.3
Advocaat		6.3	1.8
Aero, milk chocolate		31.5	9.0
After-eight mints		13.5	3.8
All-Bran	Kellogg's	2.2	0.6
Almonds, (shelled)		53.5	15.3
(shelled, roasted, salted)		57.7	16.5
(sugared)		84.4	24.1
Alpen	Weetabix	5.8	1.6
Alphabetti Spaghetti	Crosse & Blackwell	0.6	0.2
Anchovies		10.3	2.9
Angel Delight, chocolate, as served	Birds	6.7	1.9
other flavours, as served	Birds	7.0	2.0
Apple		0	0
Apple crumble	(home-made)	6.9	2.0
Apple pie (Harvest)	Lyons	14.8	4.2
Apple and Blackberry pie (Harvest)	Lyons	14.0	4.0
Apricots, fresh		Tr	Tr
Apricot pie (Harvest)	Lyons	14.0	4.0
Arrowroot		0.1	0.03
Asparagus		Tr	Tr
Aubergine		Tr	Tr
Avocado	(average)	22.2	6.3

Product	Brand/comments	Fat (g/100g)	Fat (g/oz)
Bacon (raw)		33.3	9.5
back (grilled)		33.8	9.6
back (fried)		40.6	11.6
streaky (grilled)		36.0	10.3
streaky (fried)		44.8	12.8
collar joint (boiled)		27.0	7.7
gammon joint (boiled)		18.9	5.7
Bakewell tarts	Lyons	22.0	6.3
Bananas		0.3	0.1
Baps	Hovis	3.9	1.1
bran	Mother's Pride	3.5	1.0
soft	Mother's Pride	3.1	0.9
wholemeal	Mother's Pride	3.5	1.0
wholemeal and bran	Mother's Pride	3.8	1.1
Barley, pearl (raw)		1.7	0.5
Beans, baked (canned)	(Average)	0.5	0.2
baked (canned)	Crosse & Blackwell	0.5	0.2
with pork sausages (canned)	Heinz	6.5	1.9
Beans, broad (boiled)		0.6	0.2
Beans, butter (boiled)		0.3	0.1
Beans, curried with sultanas	Heinz	1.6	0.5
Beans, French (boiled)		Tr	Tr
Beans, haricot (raw)		1.6	0.5
Beans, haricot (boiled)		0.5	0.2
Beans, mung (raw)		1.0	0.3
Beans, red kidney (raw)		1.7	0.5
Beansprouts (raw)		1.4	0.4
Beef (raw)		24.3	6.9

Product	Brand/comments	Fat (g/100g)	Fat (g/oz)
Beef, brisket (boiled, lean and fat)		23.9	6.8
fillet (fried)	Bernard Matthews	2.9	0.8
fillet, crispy crumb (fried)	Bernard Matthews	13.3	3.8
forerib (roast, lean and fat)		28.8	8.2
forerib (roast, lean only)		12.6	3.6
mince (raw)		16.2	4.6
mince (stewed)		15.2	4.3
rumpsteak (fried, lean and fat)		14.6	4.2
rumpsteak (fried, lean only)		7.4	2.1
rumpsteak (grilled, lean and fat)		12.1	3.4
rumpsteak (grilled, lean only)		6.0	1.7
salt silverside (boiled, lean and fat)		14.2	4.1
salt silverside (boiled, lean only)		4.9	1.4
sirloin (roast, lean and fat)		21.2	6.0
sirloin (roast, lean only)		9.1	2.6
roast	Bernard Matthews	9.8	2.8
roast and gravy (frozen)	Birds Eye	1.75	0.5
stewing steak (raw, lean and fat)		10.6	3.0

Product	Brand/comments	Fat (g/100g)	Fat (g/oz)
Beef, stewing steak, (stewed, lean and fat)		11.0	3.1
topside (roast, lean and fat)		12.0	3.4
topside (roast, lean only)		4.4	1.2
Beefburgers (frozen)	(average)	20.5	5.9
Beefburgers (fried)	(average)	17.3	4.9
Beefburgers, Original (frozen)	Birds Eye	20.3	5.8
Beefburgers, Original (fried)	Birds Eye	15.9	4.5
Beefburgers, 100% (frozen)	Birds Eye	30.0	8.6
Beefburgers, 100% (fried)	Birds Eye	15.9	4.5
Beefburgers, Quarterpounder (frozen)	Birds Eye	20.3	5.8
Beefburgers, Quarterpounder (fried)	Birds Eye	19.5	5.6
Beefburgers, Value (frozen)	Birds Eye	12.4	3.5
Beefburgers, Value (fried)	Birds Eye	14.3	4.1
Beef curry	Crosse & Blackwell	4.9	1.4
Beef pie, individual (frozen)	Birds Eye	4.8	1.4
Beef Stew and Dumpling (frozen)	Birds Eye	4.2	1.2
Bemax		8.1	2.3
Biscuits			
Abbey Crunch	McVitie's	17.7	5.1

Product	Brand/comments	Fat (g/100g)	Fat (g/oz)
Biscuits, Animals	Cadbury's	22.6	6.5
Bandit		30.4	8.7
Balmoral Shortbread	McVitie's	25.5	7.3
Bourbon	McVitie's	20.6	5.9
Chocolate Chip and Hazelnut Bargain Bags	McVitie's	24.2	6.9
Coconut Cookies Bargain Bags	McVitie's	26.8	7.6
Country Cookies: Almond and Honey		26.9	7.7
Cherry and Coconut		22.4	6.4
Hazelnut and Raisin		23.6	6.7
Digestive		21.9	6.3
Milk Chocolate Digestive	McVitie's	25.4	7.3
Plain Chocolate Digestive	McVitie's	25.8	7.4
Fruit Shortcake	McVitie's	21.0	6.0
Garibaldi	McVitie's	8.6	2.5
Ginger Nuts	McVitie's	14.8	4.2
Gypsy Creams	McVitie's	30.0	8.6
Jaffa Cakes	McVitie's	8.9	2.5
Lincoln	McVitie's	21.9	6.3
Marie	McVitie's	14.8	4.2
Matzo	Rakusen	1.9	0.5
Munchmallow		16.9	4.8
Orange Cremes	Cadbury's	29.5	8.4
Penguin		25.2	7.2
Rich Tea		15.6	4.9
Sports		27.6	7.9

Product	Brand/comments	Fat (g/100g)	Fat (g/oz)
Biscuits, Taxi		30.0	8.6
United		23.6	6.7
Yo Yo (mint)		27.8	7.9
Black Forest gâteau	St Ivel	11.3	3.2
Black Forest dessert	Chambourcy	3.4	1.0
Black pudding (fried)	(average)	21.9	6.3
Black pudding	Mattessons	29.0	8.3
Blancmange (as served)	Birds	3.2	0.9
Bloaters (grilled)		17.4	5.0
Bologna		27.5	7.8
Bolognese sauce	(home-made)	10.9	3.1
Bounty Bar		26.1	7.5
Bournvita (made with milk)	Cadbury's	3.7	1.1
Bovril (undiluted)		0.7	0.2
Brain, calf (boiled)		11.2	3.2
Brain, lamb (boiled)		8.8	2.5
Bran (wheat, natural)		5.5	1.6
Bran Buds	Kellogg's	1.8	0.5
Bran flakes	Kellogg's	1.1	1.3
Bratwurst	Mattessons	30.0	8.6
Brawn		11.5	3.3
Brazil nuts (shelled)		61.5	17.6
Bread, brown	(average)	2.2	0.6
brown	Nimble	2.3	0.7
country brown	Windmill	1.8	0.5
currant		3.4	1.0
Danish	Country Pride	2.2	0.6
granary	Windmill	2.1	0.6
granary wholemeal	Mother's Pride	2.5	0.7
malt		3.3	0.9

Product	Brand/comments	Fat (g/100g)	Fat (g/oz)
Bread, pumpernickel (US)		1.2	0.3
rye (US)		1.1	0.3
soda		2.3	0.7
wheatgerm	Hovis	2.5	0.7
white	(average)	1.7	0.5
white	Mother's Pride	1.5	0.4
white, high fibre	Windmill	1.9	0.5
white (fried)		37.2	10.6
white (toasted)		1.7	0.5
wholemeal	(average)	2.7	0.8
wholemeal	Windmill	2.6	0.7
wholemeal	Allinsons	2.7	0.8
wholemeal with wheatbran	Hovis	2.6	0.7
Bread roll, brown, crusty		3.2	0.9
brown, soft		6.4	1.8
starch reduced		4.1	1.2
white, crusty		3.2	0.9
white, soft		7.3	2.1
(see also baps)			
Bread and butter pudding	(home-made)	7.8	2.2
Bread sauce – see Sauces			
Brown sauce – see Sauces			
Buckwheat, whole grain	(US figs)	2.4	0.7
Buns, currant		7.6	2.2
Butter		82.0	23.4
Butterscotch	(average)	3.4	1.0
Butterscotch	Callard and Bowser	7.9	2.3

Product	Brand/comments	Fat (g/100g)	Fat (g/oz)
Cakes			
Battenburg	Lyons	10.5	3.0
Cherry Genoa	McVitie's	12.9	3.7
Chocolate cake	McVitie's	15.3	4.4
Chocolate cup cakes	Lyons	5.9	1.7
Dark Orange	McVitie's	15.0	4.3
Dundee	McVitie's	11.1	3.2
Eccles cakes	Lyons	23.3	6.7
Fancy iced	(average)	14.9	4.3
Fruit, plain	(average)	12.9	3.7
Fruit, rich	(home-made)	11.0	3.1
Fruit, rich, iced	(home-made)	11.5	3.4
Fruited tea cake	Mother's Pride	8.3	2.4
Gingerbread	(home-made)	12.6	3.6
Golden syrup	McVitie's	14.9	4.2
Jamaica Ginger	McVitie's	15.2	4.3
Kensington Slab	McVitie's	13.7	3.9
Madeira	(average)	16.9	4.8
Rock cakes		16.3	4.6
Sponge cake with fat	(creaming method)	26.5	7.6
Sponge cake without fat	(whisking method)	6.7	1.9
Swiss roll (jam)	Lyons	2.2	0.6
Swiss roll (chocolate)	Lyons	13.2	3.8
Tunis cake	McVitie's	23.1	6.6
Victoria sponge, jam-filled		4.9	1.4
Cannelloni	Crosse & Blackwell	4.1	1.2
Capers (pickled)		0	0
Captain's Pie (frozen)	Birds Eye	5.6	1.6

Product	Brand/comments	Fat (g/100g)	Fat (g/oz)
Caramac	Rowntrees	33.5	9.6
Carp (raw)		4.2	1.2
Cashew nuts (roasted & salted)	(average)	45.7	13.0
Cashew nuts	KP	47.2	13.5
Caviar		15.0	4.3
Chamby (chocolate flavour dessert)	Chambourcy	3.6	1.0
Chapatis (made with fat)		12.8	3.6
Chapatis (made without fat)		1.0	0.3
Cheese			
Austrian Smoked Cheese		24.0	6.8
Brie		23.2	6.6
Boursin, garlic		40.3	11.5
Boursin, pepper		40.3	11.5
Camembert		23.2	6.6
Cheddar		33.5	9.6
Cheddar (Tendale)	Dairy Crest	15.0	4.3
Cheshire	(average)	32.0	9.1
Cheshire (Tendale)	Dairy Crest	14.0	4.0
Cottage	(average)	4.0	1.1
Cottage cheese (natural)	St Ivel	4.2	1.2
(low fat)	Shape, St Ivel	1.5	0.4
with chives	St Ivel	4.4	1.3
with pineapple	St Ivel	3.5	1.0
with prawns	St Ivel	6.7	1.9
Cream cheese		47.4	13.5
Danish Blue		29.2	8.3
Double Gloucester		30.0	8.6

Product	Brand/comments	Fat (g/100g)	Fat (g/oz)
Cheese, Edam		22.9	6.5
Gorgonzola		26.4	7.5
Gouda		28.2	8.1
Lactic cheese	St Ivel	24.7	7.1
Lancashire		28.2	8.1
Leicester		30.0	8.6
Limburger	(US figs)	28.0	8.0
Parmesan		29.7	8.5
Processed		25.0	7.1
Roquefort	(US figs)	30.5	8.7
Shape	St Ivel	16.5	4.7
Soft cheese, full fat		21.0	6.0
low fat	Shape, St Ivel	8.8	2.5
Stilton (Blue)		40.0	11.4
St Paulin		26.2	7.5
Wensleydale		31.7	9.0
Cheese cake (cooked)	(home-made)	34.9	10.0
family size (blackcurrant)	Chambourcy	10.9	3.1
individual (blackcurrant)	Chambourcy	14.1	4.0
individual (strawberry)	Chambourcy	15.6	4.5
individual (tangy lemon)	Chambourcy	16.0	4.6
Cheese, egg and bacon flan (frozen)	Birds Eye	22.4	6.4
Cheese sauce – see Sauces			
Cheese soufflé	(home-made)	19.0	5.4
Cheese spread		22.9	6.5
Cheese straws	(home-made)	29.9	8.5

Product	Brand/comments	Fat (g/100g)	Fat (g/oz)
Cheesies (frozen)	Birds Eye	7.0	2.0
Cheesies (fried)	Birds Eye (approx)	10.0	5.0
Chestnuts		2.7	0.8
Chick peas (raw)		5.7	1.6
(cooked, dahl)		3.3	0.9
Chicken (boiled, light meat)		4.9	1.4
(boiled, dark meat)		9.9	2.8
(roast, meat and skin)		14.0	4.0
(roast, light meat)		4.0	1.1
(roast, dark meat)		6.9	1.9
(roast, and gravy (frozen)	Birds Eye	2.6	0.7
curry	Crosse & Blackwell	2.6	0.7
curry with rice (frozen)		4.0	1.1
Chicken and mushroom casserole (frozen)	Birds Eye	3.5	1.0
Chicken pie, individual (frozen)	Birds Eye	18.9	5.4
Chicken supreme with rice	Birds Eye	6.2	1.8
Chilli con carne with rice	Birds Eye	4.4	1.3
Chilli con carne	Crosse & Blackwell	1.3	0.4
Chocolate, Bournville	Cadbury's	29.6	8.4
Brazil nut	Cadbury's	35.5	10.1
Buttons	Cadbury's	29.4	8.4
Cream	Fry's	12.7	3.6
Fruit and Nut	Cadbury's	24.5	7.0
milk	(average)	30.3	8.6

Product	Brand/comments	Fat (g/100g)	Fat (g/oz)
Chocolate, Milk Tray	Cadbury's	19.7	5.6
plain	(average)	29.2	8.3
Roast Almond	Cadbury's	34.2	9.8
Wholenut	Cadbury's	36.0	10.3
Chocolate, drinking (powder)		6.0	1.7
Chocolate, drink (powder)	Carnation	5.8	1.6
Chocolate, spread	Cadbury's	2.0	0.6
Chow mein (dehydrated)	Vesta	11.6	3.3
Christmas pudding		11.6	3.3
Chutney – see Pickles			
Cockles (boiled)		0.3	0.1
Coconut (desiccated)		62.0	17.7
(fresh)		36.0	10.3
Coconut milk		24.9	7.1
Coco Pops	Kellogg's	0.9	0.3
Cod (baked)		1.2	0.3
dried and salted (soaked and boiled)		0.9	0.3
fillet (frozen)	Birds Eye	Tr	Tr
(fried in batter)		10.3	2.9
(grilled)		1.3	0.4
in butter sauce	Birds Eye	3.5	1.0
in cheese sauce	Birds Eye	4.1	1.2
in mushroom sauce	Birds Eye	5.0	1.4
in parsley sauce	Birds Eye	2.6	0.7
in shrimp flavour sauce	Birds Eye	4.1	1.2
(poached)		1.1	0.3
raw (fresh fillets)		0.7	0.2

Product	Brand/comments	Fat (g/100g)	Fat (g/oz)
Cod, raw (frozen steaks)		0.6	0.2
(smoked, poached)		1.6	0.5
(smoked, raw)		0.6	0.2
steak in breadcrumbs (frozen)	Findus	0.9	0.3
(steamed)		0.9	0.3
Cod liver oil		99.9	28.5
Cod roe (raw)		1.7	0.5
Cod roe (fried)		11.9	3.4
Coffee (instant)		0	0
Coffee and chicory essence		0.2	0.1
Coffee Compliment	Cadbury's	36.0	10.3
Coffee Mate	Carnation	34.0	9.7
Coleslaw	Mattessons	13.0	3.7
Coleslaw	St Ivel	9.5	2.7
vinaigrette	St Ivel	7.3	2.1
vinaigrette	Mattessons	2.0	0.6
with low calorie dressing	Tartan	3.5	1.0
Coley (saithe, fresh)		0.5	0.1
(steamed)		0.6	0.2
'Cook in the Pot' mixes:			
Lamb ragout	Crosse & Blackwell	12.9	3.7
Chicken chasseur	Crosse & Blackwell	19.9	5.7
Madras curry	Crosse & Blackwell	26.0	7.4
Beef goulash	Crosse & Blackwell	15.2	4.3
Beef stroganoff	Crosse & Blackwell	19.8	5.6

Product	Brand/comments	Fat (g/100g)	Fat (g/oz)
'Cook in the Pot' mixes:			
Fish bonne femme	Crosse & Blackwell	12.8	3.6
Beef carbonnade	Crosse & Blackwell	17.3	4.9
Corn, sweet (canned)		0.5	0.1
Corn on the cob (raw)		2.4	0.7
(boiled)		2.3	0.6
Corned beef (canned)	(average)	12.1	3.4
Corned beef (canned)	Libby	11.0	3.1
Cornflakes	Kellogg's	0.3	0.1
Crunchy Nut Cornflakes	Kellogg's	4.9	1.4
Cornish pasty	(average)	20.4	5.8
Cornish pasty	Findus	17.2	4.9
Cottage pie (frozen)	Findus	3.4	0.9
Country Store	Kellogg's	5.9	1.7
Country vegetable, low calorie spread	Waistline	4.8	1.4
Courgettes (frozen) fried	Birds Eye	5.3	1.5
Crab meat (boiled)		5.2	1.5
(canned)		0.9	0.3
Crackers:			
Butter puffs		23.6	6.7
Cheddars		31.9	9.1
Cheeselets	Peak Frean	16.9	4.8
Cheese Ritz	Nabisco	23.4	6.7
Cream	McVitie's	11.2	3.2
Krackawheat	Crawfords	24.9	7.1
Ritz	Nabisco	24.7	7.0
Savours		30.2	8.6
Tuc		27.6	7.9
Tuc Savoury Cream		37.0	10.6

Product	Brand/comments	Fat (g/100g)	Fat (g/oz)
Water biscuits		8.8	2.5
Cream, double (fresh)		48.2	13.8
single (fresh)		21.2	6.0
soured	St Ivel	18.0	5.1
sterilized (canned)		23.3	6.6
whipping (fresh)	St Ivel	40.0	11.4
Crème caramel, individual	St Ivel	1.7	0.5
Crisps – see Potato crisps			
Crispy Cod Fries (frozen) fried	Birds Eye	9.1	2.6
Crispbread – see brands			
Crumpets	Mother's Pride	0.6	0.2
Crunchie	Cadbury's	19.3	5.5
Cucumber (raw)		0.1	Tr
Cucumber spread	Heinz	16.9	4.8
Curly Wurly	Cadbury's	18.4	5.3
Currants (dried)		Tr	Tr
Curry powder	(average)	10.8	3.1
Custard (as served)	(average)	4.4	1.3
(ready to serve)	Birds	3.2	0.9
powder, dry weight		0.7	0.2
Custard tart	(home-made)	16.9	4.8

Product	Brand/comments	Fat (g/100g)	Fat (g/oz)
Dalky Chocolate dessert	Chambourcy	4.6	1.3
Dalky Strawberry dessert	Chambourcy	4.7	1.3
Dates (dried)		Tr	Tr
Dogfish – see Rock salmon			
Dessert Topping, Tip Top	Nestlé	6.5	1.8
Dessert Topping, Double Top	Nestlé	11.1	3.2
Discos, ready salted	KP	35.3	10.1
Double Decker	Cadbury's	18.1	5.2
Doughnut	(average)	15.8	4.5
Dream Topping, as served	Birds	13.8	3.9
Drinking Chocolate made with milk	Cadbury's	3.9	1.1
Dripping, beef		99.0	28.3
Duck (roast, meat only)		9.7	2.8
(roast, meat, fat, skin)		29.0	8.3
Dumpling		11.7	3.3
Dutch Crispbake	Nabisco	6.0	1.7

Product	Brand/comments	Fat (g/100g)	Fat (g/oz)
Eclairs (chocolate)	(average)	24.0	6.8
(chocolate, frozen)	Birds Eye	36.7	10.5
Eel (fresh)	(average)	11.3	3.2
(stewed)	(average)	13.2	3.8
Eggs, whole (raw)		10.9	3.1
whole (dried)		43.3	12.4
white		Tr	Tr
yolk		30.5	8.7
(boiled)		10.9	3.1
(fried)		19.5	5.6
(poached)		11.7	3.3
(scrambled)		22.7	6.5
duck (whole, raw)		14.5	4.1
Egg custard	(home-made)	6.0	1.7
Energen crispbread		7.6	2.2

Product	Brand/comments	Fat (g/100g)	Fat (g/oz)
Faggots	(average)	18.5	5.3
in rich sauce (frozen)	Birds Eye	11.5	3.3
Faggots 'n' Peas	Crosse & Blackwell	4.5	1.3
Fish cakes (frozen)	(average)	0.8	0.2
(fried)		10.5	3.0
cod (frozen)	Birds Eye	1.0	0.3
cod (fried)	Birds Eye (approx)	20.0	5.7
salmon (frozen)	Birds Eye	2.0	0.6
salmon (fried)	Birds Eye (approx)	22.0	6.3
savoury (frozen)	Birds Eye	1.0	0.3
savoury (fried)	Birds Eye (approx)	20.0	5.7
Fish Fingers (frozen)	(average)	7.5	2.1
(fried)	(average)	12.7	3.6
Value (frozen)	Birds Eye	8.0	2.3
(See also entries for individual types of fish)			
Fish paste	(average)	10.4	2.9
Fish paste: Anchovy		10.0	2.8
Bloater		10.0	2.8
Crab		11.0	3.1
Pilchard and Tomato		11.0	3.1
Salmon and Shrimp		12.0	3.4
Sardine and Tomato		12.0	3.4
Fish pie	(home-made)	5.7	1.6
Flake	Cadbury's	29.4	8.4
Flounder (baked)	(US figs)	8.2	2.3
Flour, plain		1.2	0.3

Product	Brand/comments	Fat (g/100g)	Fat (g/oz)
Flour, rye		2.0	0.6
self-raising		1.2	0.3
white (breadmaking)		1.2	0.3
wholemeal		2.0	0.6
Frankfurters – see Sausages			
Frosties	Kellogg's	0.2	Tr
Frog legs, raw	(US figs)	0.3	0.1
Fruit Gums		0	0
Fruit Pastilles	Rowntrees	0	0
Fruit pie, individual	(average)	15.5	4.4
pastry top	(home-made)	7.6	2.2
filling (canned)	(average)	Tr	Tr
Fudge, chocolate	Cadbury's	16.5	4.7
Vanilla flavour		11.1	3.1
Vanilla flavour with nuts		16.4	4.7
Chocolate flavour		12.2	3.5
Chocolate flavour with nuts		17.4	4.9

Product	Brand/comments	Fat (g/100g)	Fat (g/oz)
Gammon – see under Bacon, Ham			
Garlic cloves (raw)		0.2	Tr
Gelatine		Tr	Tr
Ginger (ground)		3.3	0.9
Ginger root (fresh)		1.0	0.3
Goose (roast)		22.4	6.4
Grapenuts		3.0	0.8
Green pepper		0.4	0.1
Gravy Pot (gravy concentrate)	Colman's	41.5	11.8
Grouse (roast)		5.3	1.5

Product	Brand/comments	Fat (g/100g)	Fat (g/oz)
Haddock (fresh)		0.6	0.2
(fresh, fried in breadcrumbs)		8.3	2.4
(fresh, steamed)		0.8	0.2
fillet (frozen)	Birds Eye	Tr	Tr
smoked (steamed)		0.9	0.3
smoked, buttered (frozen)	Birds Eye	3.5	1.0
in traditional batter (frozen) fried	Birds Eye	11.0	3.1
Haggis (boiled)		21.7	6.2
Halibut (fresh)		2.4	0.7
(fresh, steamed)		4.0	1.1
Hake (fresh)	(US figs)	0.4	0.1
Ham (canned)	(average)	5.1	1.4
honey roast	Mattessons	10.0	2.8
Maryland	Mattessons	2.0	0.6
Old Smokey	Mattessons	11.0	3.1
Ham and beef roll	Crosse & Blackwell	14.2	4.0
Ham and chicken roll	Crosse & Blackwell	14.5	4.1
Ham and pork (chopped)	(average)	23.6	6.7
Ham and pork (chopped)	Mattessons	30.0	8.6
Ham and tongue roll	Crosse & Blackwell	20.7	5.9
Hare (stewed)		8.0	2.3
Harvest Crunch	Quaker	19.0	5.4
Hazelnuts		36.0	10.3
Heart, lamb (raw)		5.6	1.6
ox (raw)		3.6	1.0
pig (raw)		2.7	0.8

Product	Brand/comments	Fat (g/100g)	Fat (g/oz)
Heart, sheep (roasted)		14.7	4.2
Herring (fresh)		18.5	5.3
(fried)		15.1	4.3
(grilled)		13.0	3.7
pickled (rollmop)		15.1	4.3
(smoked) – see Bloaters, Kippers			
Herring roe (raw)		3.0	0.8
(fried)		15.8	4.5
Horlicks malted milk		7.5	2.1
Hula Hoops	KP	31.9	9.1

Product	Brand/comments	Fat (g/100g)	Fat (g/oz)
Ice cream (dairy)		6.6	1.9
(non-dairy)		8.2	2.3
Instant Whip (as served)	Birds	3.5	1.0

Product	Brand/comments	Fat (g/100g)	Fat (g/oz)
Jaffa Cakes	McVitie's	8.9	2.5
Jam tarts	(home-made)	14.9	4.2
Apricot	Lyons	12.9	3.7
Raspberry	Lyons	13.4	3.8
Strawberry	Lyons	12.2	3.5
Jelly babies	Bassetts	0	0
Jelly beans	Bassetts	0	0
Jelly dessert as served (made with water)		0	0
as served (made with milk)		1.6	0.4
as sold		0	0

Product	Brand/comments	Fat (g/100g)	Fat (g/oz)
Ketchup, tomato	(average)	Tr	Tr
Ketchup, tomato	Heinz	Tr	Tr
Kidney, lamb (raw)		2.7	0.8
lamb (fried)		6.3	1.8
ox (raw)		2.6	0.7
ox (stewed)		7.7	2.2
pig (raw)		2.7	0.8
pig (stewed)		6.1	1.7
Kipper (baked)	(average)	11.4	3.2
buttered fillets (frozen)	Birds Eye	14.0	4.0
Kit-Kat	Rowntrees	27.0	7.7
Knockwurst	(US figs)	23.2	6.6

Product	Brand/comments	Fat (g/100g)	Fat (g/oz)
Lamb (lean)	(average)	8.8	2.5
breast (roast, lean and fat)		37.1	10.6
breast (roast, lean only)		16.6	4.7
chops, loin (grilled, lean and fat)		29.0	8.3
chops, loin (grilled, lean only)		12.3	3.5
leg (roast, lean and fat)		17.9	5.1
leg (roast, lean only)		8.1	2.3
scrag end neck (stewed, lean)		15.7	4.5
shoulder (roast, lean and fat)		26.3	7.5
shoulder (roast, lean only)		11.2	3.2
Lard		99.0	28.3
Lasagne	Crosse & Blackwell	5.2	1.5
(frozen)	Birds Eye	3.7	1.0
Laver bread		3.7	1.0
Lemon cheese	Hartley's	6.8	1.9
Lemon curd	(home-made)	13.5	3.8
Lemon curd	Chivers	4.6	1.3
Lemon meringue pie	(home-made)	14.6	4.2
Lentils (dried)		1.0	0.3
Lettuce (raw)		0.4	0.1
Lion Bar	Rowntrees	24.0	6.8
Liquorice allsorts		2.2	0.6
Liver, calf (raw)		7.3	2.1
calf (fried)		13.2	3.8

Product	Brand/comments	Fat (g/100g)	Fat (g/oz)
Liver, chicken (raw)		6.3	1.8
chicken (fried)		10.9	3.1
lamb (raw)		10.3	2.9
lamb (fried)		14.0	4.0
ox (raw)		7.8	2.2
ox (stewed)		9.5	2.7
pig (raw)		6.8	1.9
pig (stewed)		8.1	2.3
Liver sausage	(average)	26.9	7.7
Liver sausage	Mattessons	20.0	5.7
Liverwurst (smoked)		27.4	7.8
Lobster (boiled)		3.4	1.0
Low fat spread	Outline	39.5	11.3
Low fat spread	St Ivel Gold	39.0	11.1
Luncheon meat	(average)	26.9	7.7
Luncheon meat, pork	Mattessons	27.0	7.7

Product	Brand/comments	Fat (g/100g)	Fat (g/oz)
Macaroni (raw)		2.0	0.6
(boiled)		0.6	0.2
Macaroni cheese	(home-made)	9.7	2.8
Macaroni cheese	Heinz	7.0	2.0
Macaroni cheese	Crosse & Blackwell	5.9	1.7
Mackerel (fresh)		16.3	4.6
(fried)		11.3	3.2
fillets	Libby	10.0	2.8
MacVita	McVitie's	13.7	3.9
Maltesers		24.6	7.0
Maple syrup	(US figs)	0	0
Marathon	Mars	27.6	7.9
Margarine		81.0	23.1
Marmite		0.7	0.2
Mars Bar		19.5	5.6
Marshmallows		Tr	Tr
Marzipan	(home-made)	24.9	7.1
Matchmakers, coffee flavour	Rowntrees	24.5	7.0
mint flavour		22.0	6.3
orange flavour		23.5	6.7
Mayonnaise	(home-made)	78.9	22.5
Mayonnaise	Hellman's	78.0	22.3
Mayonnaise	Waistline	38.4	10.9
Meat paste	(average)	11.2	3.5
Beef	Shippams	12.0	3.4
Chicken	Shippams	16.0	4.6
Ham and beef	Shippams	12.0	3.4
Meringues		0	0
Milk, coconut		0.2	Tr

Product	Brand/comments	Fat (g/100g)	Fat (g/oz)
Milk, condensed sweetened (whole)		9.0	2.6
condensed sweetened (skimmed)		0.3	0.1
dried whole		26.3	7.5
dried	Five Pints	2.4	0.7
dried, reconstituted	Marvel	0.2	Tr
evaporated	Carnation	9.0	2.6
fresh (whole)		3.8	1.1
fresh (skimmed)		0.1	Tr
goat's		4.5	1.3
human (10 days after childbirth)		3.7	1.1
human (1 month after childbirth)		4.1	1.2
low fat	Shape, St Ivel	1.0	0.3
sterilised		3.8	1.1
UHT treated		3.8	1.1
Milk Tray	Cadbury's	19.7	5.6
Milky Way	Mars	17.0	4.8
Mincemeat	(average)	4.3	1.2
Mincemeat	Hartley's	3.9	1.1
Mince pie	(home-made)	20.7	5.9
Mince pie	Lyons	17.2	4.9
Mince savour	Crosse & Blackwell	6.0	1.7
bolognese mix	Crosse & Blackwell	9.2	2.6
burger mix	Crosse & Blackwell	6.8	1.9
Minstrels	Mars	24.8	7.1
Miso		4.6	1.3

Product	Brand/comments	Fat (g/100g)	Fat (g/oz)
Mortadella	(US figs)	25.0	7.1
Mousse, fruit	St Ivel	7.6	2.2
chocolate	St Ivel	7.9	2.3
Muesli	(average)	7.5	2.1
Muffins	Mother's Pride	2.2	0.6
wholewheat and bran	Hovis	2.5	0.7
Mullet (raw)		6.9	1.9
Murray Mints	Pascall	5.4	1.5
Mushroom (fresh)		0.6	0.2
(fried)		22.3	6.4
Mussels (raw)		1.9	0.5
(boiled)		2.0	0.6
Mustard, English	Colman's	9.5	2.7
Mustard powder		28.7	8.2

Product	Brand/comments	Fat (g/100g)	Fat (g/oz)
Noodles, Doodle	Heinz	0.6	0.2
(*See also* Macaroni, Spaghetti			
Norfolk Burger (2oz) (fried)	Bernard Matthews	16.1	4.6
Nuts, mixed, and raisins	KP	30.0	8.6
mixed, salted	Sun Pat	50.5	14.4

(*See also* nuts by individual name)

Product	Brand/comments	Fat (g/100g)	Fat (g/oz)
Oatcakes		18.3	5.2
Oat Crunchies	Quaker	5.6	1.6
Oatmeal (raw)		8.7	2.5
Oil, salad		100	28.5
Olives in brine (flesh only)		11	3.1
Onions (raw)		Tr	Tr
(fried)		33.3	9.5
Onion and Chives, low calorie spread	Waistline	4.7	1.3
Onions, small, in white sauce	Birds Eye	8.4	2.4
Outline – see Low fat spread			
Original Crunchy bar with apple and bran	Jordan's	18.0	5.1
Oxo beef drink		0.2	Tr
Oxo cubes, beef		3.4	1.0
chicken		4.5	1.3
Oxtail (raw)		10.1	2.9
(stewed)		13.4	3.8
Oysters (raw)		0.9	0.3

Product	Brand/comments	Fat (g/100g)	Fat (g/oz)
Paella	Crosse & Blackwell	9.0	2.6
(frozen)	Birds Eye	1.4	0.4
Pancakes	(home-made)	16.3	4.6
Scotch	(home-made)	11.6	3.3
Patrtridge (roast)		7.2	2.0
Pastry, choux (raw)	(home-made)	13.0	3.7
choux (cooked)	(home-made)	20.1	5.7
flaky (raw)	(home-made)	30.6	8.7
flaky (cooked)	(home-made)	40.5	11.6
puff (frozen)	Birds Eye	28.0	8.0
shortcrust (raw)	(home-made)	27.8	7.9
shortcrust (cooked)	(home-made)	32.2	9.2
shortcrust (frozen)	Birds Eye	28.0	8.0
Pâté, Ardennes	Mattessons	35.0	10.0
Brussels	Mattessons	38.0	10.8
Ham & Tongue	Mattessons	15.0	4.3
Liver	Mattessons	27.0	7.7
Liver & Bacon	Mattessons	26.0	7.4
Liver & Ham	Mattessons	25.0	7.1
Turkey	Mattessons	29.0	8.3
Peanut butter, smooth	(average)	53.7	15.3
Peanut butter, smooth	Sun Pat	50.0	14.3
crunchy	Sun Pat	50.0	14.3
Peanut brittle	(average)	10.4	2.9
Peanuts, fresh		24.3	6.9
roasted and salted	KP	49.4	14.1
roasted and salted	Sun Pat	50.5	14.4
and raisins	KP	24.7	7.0
Peas, fresh, frozen or processed		0.4	0.1

Product	Brand/comments	Fat (g/100g)	Fat (g/oz)
Peas, split, dried (raw)		1.0	0.3
split, dried (boiled)		0.3	0.1
red pigeon (raw)		2.0	0.6
Pepper		6.5	1.8
Peppermints	Polo	1.2	0.3
Peppermint Cream	Fry's	13.8	3.9
Pheasant (roast)		9.3	2.6
Piccalilli	(average)	0.7	0.2
Piccalilli	Heinz	0.6	0.1
Piccalilli	Haywards	0.3	0.1
Pickles: Apple chutney	(home-made)	0.1	Tr
Branston pickle		0	0
Cucumber chutney	Sharwood	Tr	Tr
Mango & ginger chutney	Sharwood	0	0
Pickled onions		0	0
Ploughman's	Heinz	0.2	Tr
Sweet military	Haywards	0.4	0.1
Tomato chutney	(home-made)	0.1	Tr
Picnic bar	Cadbury's	29.6	8.5
Pigeon (roast)		13.2	3.8
Pilchards (canned) in tomato sauce		5.4	1.5
Pistachio nuts, salted	(US figs)	53.7	15.3
Pizza, cheese and tomato	(home-made)	11.5	3.3
tomato and cheese (frozen)	Birds Eye	12.9	3.7
ham and mushroom (frozen)	Birds Eye	10.6	3.0
Plaice (raw)		2.2	0.6
in crisp crunch crumb (fried)	Birds Eye	17.5	5.0

Product	Brand/comments	Fat (g/100g)	Fat (g/oz)
Plaice, crispy fillet (fried)	Birds Eye	14.0	4.0
crispy whole (fried)	Birds Eye	14.0	4.0
in batter (fried)		18.0	5.1
in breadcrumbs (fried)		13.7	3.9
(steamed)		1.9	0.5
Plantain (raw)		0.2	Tr
(boiled)		0.1	Tr
(fried)		9.2	2.6
Polony	(average)	21.1	6.0
Polony	Mattessons	18.0	5.1
Popcorn, salted	(US figs)	21.8	6.2
Popcorn, sweet	(US figs)	3.5	1.0
Pork belly rashers (raw)		35.5	10.1
belly rashers (grilled)		34.8	9.9
chops (raw, lean and fat)		29.5	8.4
chops (grilled, lean and fat)		24.2	6.9
chops (grilled, lean only)		10.7	3.0
leg (roast, lean and fat)		19.8	5.6
leg (roast, lean only)		6.9	1.9
Pork and pepper loaf	Mattessons	20.0	5.7
Pork pie, individual	(average)	27.0	7.7
Pork roll, stuffed	Tyne Brand	11.9	3.4
Porridge, as served		0.9	0.3
Porridge oats		8.7	2.5
Potato, instant (dry weight)	(average)	0.8	0.2
instant (dry weight)	Wondermash	1.1	0.3
instant (made up as directed)	(average)	0.2	Tr

Product	Brand/comments	Fat (g/100g)	Fat (g/oz)
Potato, instant (made up as directed)	Cadbury's Smash	0.1	Tr
chips	(home-made)	10.9	3.1
chips (frozen)	(average)	3.0	0.8
chips (fried)	(average)	18.9	5.4
chips (frozen, fried)	Birds Eye	14.0	4.0
chips, oven (frozen, baked)	Birds Eye	7.0	2.0
chips, oven ready	McCain	6.2	1.8
chips, oven ready (grilled)	McCain	5.2	1.5
crisps, mixed	(average)	35.9	7.4
crisps, ready salted	KP	37.7	10.8
Crispy Fritters (fried)	Birds Eye	12.3	3.0
Croquettes (frozen)	Birds Eye	30.8	8.8
new, fresh (boiled)		0.1	Tr
new (canned)	(average)	0.1	Tr
new (canned)	Hartley's	0	0
old (boiled)		0.1	Tr
old (baked)		0.1	Tr
old (mashed)		5.0	1.4
old (roast)		4.8	1.4
salad (canned)	Heinz	15.0	4.3
salad, ready made	Mattessons	12.0	3.4
sticks	Smith's	23.9	6.8
Mini Waffles (fried)	Birds Eye	9.4	2.7
Pot Noodles	Knorr	20.0	5.7
Prawns, fresh (boiled)		1.8	0.5
Prawn cocktail/salad (ready made)	Eden Vale	11.3	3.2
Prawn cocktail/salad (ready made)	Mattessons	13.0	3.7

Product	Brand/comments	Fat (g/100g)	Fat (g/oz)
Prawn salad	St Ivel	12.1	3.5
Prawn curry with rice (frozen)	Birds Eye	4.0	1.1
Pretzels	(US figs)	4.5	1.3
Puffa Puffa Rice	Kellogg's	9.6	2.7
Puffed Wheat	Quaker	1.3	0.4

Product	Brand/comments	Fat (g/100g)	Fat (g/oz)
Quail (raw)	(US figs)	7.0	2.0
Queen of Puddings	(home-made)	7.9	2.3
Quiche Lorraine	(home-made)	28.1	8.0
Quick Lunch, various flavours	KP	0.1	Tr
Quinces	(US figs)	0.1	Tr

Product	Brand/comments	Fat (g/100g)	Fat (g/oz)
Rabbit (raw)		4.0	1.1
(stewed)		7.7	2.2
Rancheros	KP	21.3	6.1
Ravioli in tomato sauce (canned)	Heinz	2.5	0.7
Ready Brek	Lyons	8.7	2.5
Refreshers	Trebor	1.8	0.5
Relishes: Corn	Crosse & Blackwell	Tr	Tr
Onion	Crosse & Blackwell	0	0
Tomato	Crosse & Blackwell	Tr	Tr
Tomato and pepper	Crosse & Blackwell	0.8	0.2
Revels	Mars	26.9	7.7
Rice (boiled)		0.3	0.1
(boil in the bag)	Kellogg's	1.4	0.4
brown (raw)		1.9	0.5
brown (boiled)		0.6	0.2
polished (raw)		1.0	0.3
Rice & Things (made up as on packet) Savoury curried rice	Crosse & Blackwell	0.7	0.2
Savoury rice and mushrooms	Crosse & Blackwell	0.7	0.2
Savoury rice and peppers	Crosse & Blackwell	0.8	0.2
Savoury rice and vegetables	Crosse & Blackwell	0.8	0.2
Rice Crispies	Kellogg's	0.3	0.1
Rice pudding (canned)	(average)	2.5	0.7
Rice pudding (canned)	Heinz	1.5	0.4

Product	Brand/comments	Fat (g/100g)	Fat (g/oz)
Rice pudding, creamed (canned)	Libby	2.8	0.8
Ricicles	Kellogg's	0.2	Tr
Rissoles, Savoury (frozen)	Birds Eye	21.2	6.0
(fried)	Birds Eye	24.7	7.0
Rock salmon (dogfish) fried in batter		18.8	5.4
Rolo	Rowntrees	21.0	6.0
Rye flour		2.0	0.6
Ryking brown rye		1.7	0.5
Ryking golden wheat		6.2	1.8
Ryking Fibre plus		6.0	1.7
Ryvita (original)		3.1	0.9
(Danish style)		3.1	0.9
(Swedish style)		3.1	0.9

Product	Brand/comments	Fat (g/100g)	Fat (g/oz)
Sago (raw)		0.2	Tr
Salad cream	Heinz	27.4	7.8
Salad cream	Crosse & Blackwell	32.0	9.1
Salad dressings: French dressing	(home-made)	73.0	20.8
French dressing	Heinz	54.6	15.6
Oil-free French dressing	Waistline	0.7	0.2
Vinegar and oil dressing	Waistline	13.0	3.7
Salads, prepared: Florida	St Ivel	6.8	1.9
Spanish	Eden Vale	8.5	2.4
Waldorf	St Ivel	11.3	3.2
Salami	(average)	45.2	12.9
Salmon (canned)	(average)	8.2	2.3
(fresh)		12.0	3.4
(fresh, steamed)		13.0	3.7
(smoked)		4.5	1.3
Sandwich Spread	Heinz	18.2	5.2
Sardines in oil (canned, fish only)		13.6	3.9
in tomato sauce (canned)		11.6	3.3
Sauce, basquaise	Bonne Cuisine	12.1	3.4
bolognese	Crosse & Blackwell	3.3	0.1
bread	(home-made)	5.0	0.9
brown	Daddies	Tr	Tr
brown	HP	Tr	Tr
brown, fruity	Branston	0	0

Product	Brand/comments	Fat (g/100g)	Fat (g/oz)
Sauce, chasseur	Bonne Cuisine	9.0	2.6
cheese	(home-made)	14.6	4.2
cheese (pour over)	Crosse & Blackwell	7.6	2.2
hollandaise	Bonne Cuisine	15.4	4.4
horseradish		10.6	3.0
onion	(home-made)	6.4	1.8
seafood	Waistline	12.5	3.6
soy (see Soy sauce)			
sweet and sour	Crosse & Blackwell	1.4	0.4
tartare	Waistline	11.0	3.1
tartare	Sharwood	18.0	5.1
tomato (see Ketchup)			
white savoury	(home-made)	10.3	2.9
white savoury, dry mix	Colman's	9.7	2.8
white sweet	(home-made)	9.5	2.7
Worcestershire	Lea and Perrins	0.5	0.1
Sausage, garlic	Mattessons	19.0	5.4
Sausage roll (flaky pastry)	(home-made)	36.2	10.3
(shortcrust pastry)	(home-made)	31.8	9.1
(frozen)	Findus	18.0	5.1
Sausages, beef (raw)		24.1	6.9
beef (fried)		18.0	5.1
beef (grilled)		17.3	4.9
frankfurter	(average)	25.0	7.1
frankfurter	Mattessons	32.0	9.1
German	Mattessons	19.0	5.4
ham	Mattessons	6.0	1.7

Product	Brand/comments	Fat (g/100g)	Fat (g/oz)
Sausages, pork (raw)		32.1	9.2
pork (fried)		24.5	7.0
pork (grilled)		24.6	7.0
pork and beef		24.7	7.1
smoked	Bernard Matthews	24.9	7.1
turkey with pork (fried)	Bernard Matthews	20.5	5.8
turkey with pork (grilled)		19.7	5.6
Saveloy	(average)	20.5	5.8
Scallops (steamed)		1.4	0.4
in breadcrumbs (frozen, fried)		8.4	2.4
Scampi (frozen) in breadcrumbs (fried)		17.6	5.0
Scones	(home-made)	14.6	4.2
sultana	Mother's Pride	10.4	2.9
Scotch Egg	(average)	20.9	5.9
Scotch pancakes – see Pancakes			
Semolina (raw)		1.8	0.5
Semolina pudding, creamed	Heinz	1.7	0.5
Sesame seeds		49.1	14.0
Shepherds pie (frozen)	Birds Eye	6.6	1.9
Sherbet lemons	Trebor	0	0
Shortbread	(home-made)	26.0	7.4
Shortbread	Crawfords	25.9	7.4
Shredded Wheat	Nabisco	2.3	0.6
Shreddies	Nabisco	1.9	0.5
Shrimps (boiled)		2.4	0.7

Product	Brand/comments	Fat (g/100g)	Fat (g/oz)
Shrimps (canned)		1.2	0.3
Silverside	Mattessons	6.0	1.7
Skate in batter (fried)		12.1	3.4
Slender (powder) Chocolate flavour	Carnation	2.4	0.7
Other flavours	Carnation	0.7	0.2
Yoghurt enriched	Carnation	3.5	1.0
Slender bars, chocolate/ coffee flavour	Carnation	21.0	6.0
Slender crunch bars	Carnation	28.0	8.0
Slimway Low Calorie Dressing	Heinz	8.7	2.5
Smarties	Rowntrees	17.5	5.0
Snackpots, Curry & Rice with Beef	Batchelors	5.9	1.7
Curry & Rice with Chicken	Batchelors	3.0	0.8
Snapper, red (fresh)	(US figs)	0.9	0.3
Sole, lemon in breadcrumbs (fried)		13.0	3.7
(steamed)		0.9	0.3
Sorbet, lemon	Walls	0	0
Soufflé, cheese	(home-made)	19.0	5.4
Soups: Beef & tomato (dry)	Batchelors Cup-a-Soup	6.8	1.9
Beef broth (canned)	Heinz	0.5	0.1
Chicken noodle (dried), as served	(average)	0.3	0.1
Chicken noodle (dry)	Batchelors	2.7	0.8
Cream of Celery (canned)	Heinz	3.5	1.0
Cream of Chicken (canned)	(average)	3.8	1.1

Product	Brand/comments	Fat (g/100g)	Fat (g/oz)
Soup, Cream of Chicken (canned)	Crosse & Blackwell	4.4	1.2
Cream of Chicken (canned, condensed)	(average)	7.2	2.0
Cream of Chicken (condensed, as served)	(average)	3.6	1.0
Cream of Mushroom (canned)	(average)	3.8	1.1
Cream of Mushroom (canned)	Crosse & Blackwell	3.6	1.0
Cream of Mushroom (canned)	Heinz	4.2	1.2
Cream of Tomato (canned)	(average)	3.3	0.9
Cream of Tomato (canned)	Heinz	3.5	1.0
Cream of Tomato (canned, condensed)	(average)	6.8	1.9
Cream of Tomato (condensed, as served)	(average)	3.4	1.0
Consommé (canned)	Crosse & Blackwell	0	0
Country vegetable with beef (canned)	Crosse & Blackwell	0.6	0.2
Farmhouse thick vegetable (canned)	Crosse & Blackwell	1.0	0.3
French onion	Crosse & Blackwell	0.6	0.2
Lentil	(home-made)	3.7	1.1
Lentil (canned)	Heinz	1.3	0.4
Lobster bisque	Crosse & Blackwell	1.1	0.3

Product	Brand/comments	Fat (g/100g)	Fat (g/oz)
Soup, Minestrone (canned)	Heinz	0.9	0.3
Minestrone (dried, made as directed)	(average)	0.7	0.2
Minestrone (dry)	Knorr	8.0	2.3
Mulligatawny (canned)	Heinz	3.3	0.9
Oxtail (dried, made as directed)	(average)	0.8	0.2
Oxtail (dry)	Batchelors Cup-a-Soup	8.2	2.3
Oxtail (canned)	(average)	1.7	0.5
Oxtail (canned)	Heinz	1.6	0.4
Pea, thick (dry)	Batchelors	8.2	2.3
Pea & ham (canned)	Heinz	1.8	0.5
Scotch broth (canned)	Heinz	0.7	0.2
Scottish lentil with vegetable	Crosse & Blackwell	1.0	0.3
Tomato (dried, made as directed)	(average)	0.5	0.1
Vegetable (canned)	(average)	0.7	0.2
Vegetable (canned)	Heinz	0.7	0.2
Vegetable & beef (canned) Low calorie	Heinz	0.4	0.1
Vegetable (spring)	Heinz	0.9	0.3
Vichyssoise	Crosse & Blackwell	3.1	0.9
Soya bean curd	(US figs)	4.2	1.2
Soya beans (dried)	(US figs)	17.7	5.1
Soya beans (cooked)	(US figs)	5.7	1.6
Soya beans (canned)	(US figs)	5.0	1.4
Soya bean milk, liquid	(US figs)	1.5	0.4
Soya flour (full fat)		23.5	6.7

Product	Brand/comments	Fat (g/100g)	Fat (g/oz)
Soya flour (low fat)		7.2	2.0
Soy, sauce		1.3	0.4
Spaghetti (raw)		1.0	0.3
Spaghetti (boiled)		0.3	0.1
Spaghetti bolognese (canned)	Heinz	3.0	0.8
(*See also* bolognese sauce, home-made)			
Spaghetti in tomato sauce (canned)	(average)	0.7	0.2
Spaghetti in tomato sauce (canned)	Heinz	0.5	0.1
Spaghetti hoops in tomato sauce (canned)	Heinz	0.3	0.1
Spaghetti rings (canned)	Crosse & Blackwell	0.5	0.1
Spaghetti shells in tomato sauce (canned)	Heinz	1.6	0.4
Special K	Kellogg's	0.3	0.1
Spicy vegetable, low calorie spread	Waistline	4.4	1.2
Spinach (boiled)		0.5	0.1
Sponge pudding (steamed)	home-made	16.4	4.7
chocolate (canned)	Heinz	13.2	3.8
treacle (canned)	Heinz	9.6	2.7
Sprats, fresh (fried)		37.9	10.8
Star Bar	Cadbury's	29.7	8.5
Steak – see Beef			
Steakhouse grill, beef (frozen)	Birds Eye	25.2	7.2
Steakhouse grill, beef (grilled)	Birds Eye	19.1	5.4

Product	Brand/comments	Fat (g/100g)	Fat (g/oz)
Steak, stewed with gravy (canned)	(average)	12.5	3.6
Steak & Kidney pie (pastry top only)	(home-made)	18.3	5.2
individual	(average)	21.2	6.1
(canned)	Fray Bentos	12.1	3.5
(canned)	Tyne Brand	11.8	3.4
(frozen)	Findus	12.0	3.4
filling	Fray Bentos	10.0	2.8
Steak & Kidney pudding	Tyne Brand	14.2	4.0
Steak & onion pie filling (canned)	Tyne Brand	5.8	1.7
Steak pie filling, stewed (canned)	Tyne Brand	6.2	1.8
Stock cubes, beef	Knorr	20.0	5.7
chicken	Knorr	22.5	6.4
Sturgeon (steamed)	(US figs)	5.7	1.6
Suet, block		99.0	28.3
shredded		86.7	24.8
Suet pudding (steamed)	(home-made)	18.1	5.2
Sugar Puffs	Quaker	1.0	0.3
Sugar Smacks	Kellogg's	2.1	0.6
Sultana Bran	Kellogg's	0.8	0.2
Sunflower seeds	(US figs)	47.3	13.5
Super Noodles (made as directed)	Kellogg's	6.9	1.9
Sweetbreads lamb (raw)		7.8	2.2
Sweetbreads lamb (fried)		14.6	4.2
Sweetcorn – see Corn			
Sweet potatoes (raw)		0.6	0.2
(boiled)		0.6	0.2

Product	Brand/comments	Fat (g/100g)	Fat (g/oz)
Tapioca (raw)		0.1	Tr
Tapioca pudding	(home-made)	4.2	1.2
Tea, liquid infusion		Tr	Tr
Toad in the hole (frozen)	Findus	11.1	3.2
Toast Topper, chicken and mushroom	Heinz	3.6	1.0
ham and cheese	Heinz	13.7	3.9
mushroom and bacon	Heinz	8.5	2.4
turkey and ham	Heinz	5.9	1.7
pizza	Heinz	2.6	0.7
Toffees, mixed	(average)	17.2	4.9
coffee	Rowntrees	18.5	5.3
Tofu – see Soya bean curd			
Tomatoes (raw)		Tr	Tr
(fried)		5.9	1.7
(canned)		Tr	Tr
Tongue, lamb (raw)		14.6	4.2
lamb (canned)		20.3	5.8
lunch	Mattessons	12.0	3.4
ox (pickled raw)		17.5	5.0
ox (boiled)		23.9	6.8
sheep (stewed)		24.0	6.9
Topic	Mars	28.6	8.2
Tortellini	Crosse & Blackwell	4.0	1.1
Treacle tart	(home-made)	14.0	4.0
Treats, peanut	Mars	28.4	8.1
toffee	Mars	17.6	5.0
Trifle sponges	Lyons	1.4	0.4
Tripe (dressed)		2.5	0.7

Product	Brand/comments	Fat (g/100g)	Fat (g/oz)
Tripe (stewed)		4.5	1.3
Trout, brown (steamed)		4.5	1.3
Tuna (canned) in oil		22.0	6.3
Turkey (roast, meat and skin)		6.5	1.8
(roast, light meat)		1.4	0.4
(roast, dark meat)		4.1	1.2
breast (roast)	Bernard Matthews	9.5	2.7
leg (roast)	Bernard Matthews	8.8	2.5
Turkey steaks (fried)	Bernard Matthews	9.3	2.6
Turkey steaks, gammon style (fried)	Bernard Matthews	14.5	4.1
Turkey steaks, crispy crumb (fried)	Bernard Matthews	17.0	4.8
Turkey burger, crispy crumb (fried)	Bernard Matthews	21.0	6.0
Turkey and ham loaf	Mattessons	14.0	4.0
Turkish Delight	Fry's	8.3	2.4
Turnips (raw/boiled)		0.3	0.1
Twiglets	Peak Freans	13.8	3.9

Product	Brand/comments	Fat (g/100g)	Fat (g/oz)
Veal, cutlet (fried)		8.1	2.3
fillet (raw)		2.7	0.8
fillet (fried)		11.5	3.3
jellied (canned)		2.8	0.8
Vegetable salad	Eden Vale	9.4	2.7
Vegetable salad (canned)	Heinz	9.8	2.8
Venison (roast)		6.4	1.8

Product	Brand/comments	Fat (g/100g)	Fat (g/oz)
Walnuts, fresh		51.5	14.7
Walnut Whip, milk chocolate	Rowntrees	24.0	6.8
Weetabix		2.0	0.6
Weetaflakes		2.0	0.6
Welsh rarebit	(home-made)	23.6	6.7
Whale meat	(US figs)	7.5	2.1
Wheat germ		10.9	3.1
Whelks (boiled)		1.9	0.5
Whitebait (fried)		47.5	13.6
White pudding	(average)	31.8	9.1
Whiting (fried)		10.3	2.9
(steamed)		0.9	0.3
Winkles		1.4	0.4

Product	Brand/comments	Fat (g/100g)	Fat (g/oz)
Yam (raw)		0.2	Tr
(boiled)		0.1	Tr
Yeast, bakers' compressed		0.4	0.1
bakers' dried		1.5	0.4
extract – see Marmite			
Yoghurt, black cherry	Ski	0.7	0.2
chocolate	Eden Vale	1.3	0.3
fruit	(average)	1.0	0.3
hazelnut	(average)	2.6	0.7
lemon fruit curd	Chambourcy	2.0	0.6
low calorie: black cherry	Waistline	0.1	Tr
natural	Waistline	0.1	Tr
prune	Waistline	0.2	Tr
strawberry	Waistline	0.1	Tr
muesli	St Ivel	1.6	0.4
natural	(average)	1.0	0.3
natural	Chambourcy	1.2	0.3
natural with honey	Eden Vale	0.9	0.2
orange	Ski	0.7	0.2
raspberry	Eden Vale	0.7	0.2
strawberry	Ski	0.7	0.2
whole milk	Chambourcy	2.5	0.7
Yoghurt dressing	Heinz	25.7	7.3
Yorkie, milk chocolate	Rowntrees	30.5	8.7
Yorkshire pudding	(home-made)	10.1	2.9

Low fat cooking

You have probably already taken the first step towards reducing the amount of fat you eat, by looking up some of your favourite foods in the listings and seeing just how much fat they contain. You may have had some surprises – and clearly any serious attempt to change your eating habits will involve a switch from higher fat foods to alternatives with a lower fat content. But since the way food is cooked can make such a difference, you may also need to rethink the way you prepare dishes and adjust some favourite recipes so that they contain less fat. Here are some suggestions which may help.

Choosing to eat less fat

There are many ways individuals can cut down on their fat consumption, and it's a matter of finding the changes which suit you best. Many people, for example, are changing to skimmed or semi-skimmed milk instead of using whole milk. And as it does not mean a change in habits, just the product used, this can be a fairly easy step.

When it comes to red meat, with its 'invisible fat', there are several possibilities. The first is to choose lean meat and also reduce the portion size. This can be done almost unnoticeably if you are making dishes where meat is already combined with vegetables or pasta, like casseroles or spaghetti bolognese. So those are the sort of dishes to go for (bearing in mind the cooking tips in the next section).

Better still, choose fish, chicken or turkey more often,

since they have less fat than red meats. And when you are having cheese, think carefully about the type you choose, or take advantage of the fact that several manufacturers are now making traditional style Cheddars with a much lower fat content.

There are some sorts of food that it is best to limit altogether. Many snack foods, with their high fat and salt content are really a bit of a hazard to the careful 'fat-watcher', especially as you get little else of nutritional value – just lots of calories. Baked goods are also something to eat in moderation, whether they are sweet like biscuits or savoury like sausage rolls.

Cooking tips

Choosing a cooking method like frying can add considerably to the amount of fat you eat. So try to limit the number of times you reach for the frying pan, unless of course it's a non-stick pan and you plan to dry-fry your food. There are better alternatives. Try grilling, or using foil to cook fish, poultry and meat in their own juices.

When making stews or casseroles, remember to skim off the fat. This is easier if the dish is allowed to cool – it can always be reheated quickly before serving. When using minced meat, as in the sauce for spaghetti bolognese, the fat which accumulates after the meat has been browned can be drained off before the tomatoes or other ingredients are added.

Adjusting recipes

If you are going to fry, then choose an oil which is low in saturated fat. In fact you should generally use a fat of this type in cooking. When making cakes and biscuits, convert your own solid fat recipes. As you will need between a quarter and a third less corn oil than butter or margarine, the total fat content will also be reduced. You may want to make some other changes in old recipes as well. Can the amount of meat in a savoury dish be reduced and other ingredients like vegetables increased? What about the cheese in your recipe? Could you change to a lower fat variety? It might be better to use a smaller quantity of a strongly-flavoured cheese than lots of mild Cheddar. You could also reduce the amount by adding a little dry mustard to boost the cheesy flavour. Dishes with rich sauces are often high in fat, but the cream or sour cream used in many recipes can be replaced with plain, low-fat, yoghurt.

Eating less fat

There are still more things that you can do to cut your fat down, even when you get to the table. The most obvious is to trim off any visible fat on the meat served. Don't forget that there is also fat attached to the skin of chicken and turkey, so it's best to remove the skin and discard it. If you are eating bread, cut the slice thickly and spread the butter or margarine thinly.

In recent years the fashion has been for more and more vegetables to appear on the table smothered in melted butter. You probably will not be doing this yourself any more, but don't be tempted to add butter once the vegetables are on your plate. When it comes to something like a baked potato, it is quite possible to combine it with a tasty mixture of cottage cheese or plain yoghurt and chives, rather than adding lashings of butter.

Of course, for many people, eating less fat means that they should be eating more of other foods to make up the calories – eating more fresh fruit, vegetables and wholegrain cereal products.

Finally, there is one fried food we all enjoy eating and will probably continue to do so, though perhaps not so often. Chips. But if you are going to make chips, there are ways in which you can improve them. Remember to cut thick chips and fry them in *hot* oil. That will keep down the fat content. Don't forget to drain them well and blot them on kitchen paper. And choose the right oil for cooking – one which is low in saturated fat, such as corn oil, sunflower or safflower oil.

By gradually introducing some of these changes the amount of fat you eat can be brought down to a healthy level – and you may be surprised how easy it is.

Footnotes on cholesterol

At one time research seemed to point to cholesterol as an important dietary factor in heart disease. Scientists found that communities where people had high levels of cholesterol in their blood also had high rates of heart disease. And when the material which clogs up people's arteries was analysed it was found to contain cholesterol. Many people became very anxious about the amount of cholesterol in their food. However, further research has shown that blood cholesterol levels are not just a simple reflection of the amount eaten.

Firstly, our bodies need cholesterol and we make much of what we need ourselves. But since we also take in cholesterol in our food, the body has a regulating mechanism to make adjustments and keep the level in our blood fairly constant. But this system can fail to function properly and it may be upset by a diet which contains too much saturated fat. Under these circumstances your doctor may advise you to follow a low cholesterol diet. In order to do this you will need to know something about the cholesterol content of different foods, which is why this additional listing has been included. For most of us it is much more important to think about out total fat intake and the proportion of that which is saturated fat rather than worry about cholesterol. The US dietary goals suggest that cholesterol consumption should be reduced to 300mg per day. However, average intake in the UK is already lower than in the US, between 350 and 450mg per day and this figure is likely to drop anyway if the saturated fat in the diet is reduced.

Most of the cholesterol which the average person eats comes from meat and dairy foods. Although shellfish and offal are concentrated sources, people tend to eat much less of these foods. Nearly all animal foods contain some cholesterol, whereas there is none in plant foods.

If you have been advised to follow a low cholesterol diet then remember:

Cut down on fat
- use low fat alternatives – see guide
- use cooking methods like grilling, braising and stewing
- fry only occasionally

Replace saturated fats with polyunsaturated fats
- if you eat cakes and pastry bake them yourself using corn oil
- if you fry use corn oil instead of dripping or lard
- blended vegetable oils may contain a higher proportion of saturated fatty acids. Use only pure oils such as corn oil or sunflower seed oil.
- use polyunsaturated margarine instead of butter

Avoid foods high in cholesterol
- restrict all shellfish, shrimps, oyster, lobster and fish roe
- avoid offal meats such as liver, pâté, kidney, heart and brain.

Summary guide to fat and cholesterol

AVOID:		REPLACE WITH:	
Foods high in saturated fat and/or cholesterol	Foods high in cholesterol	Low fat/low cholesterol alternatives	Foods high in 'polyunsaturated fat' and low in cholesterol
milk, yoghurt, cream, hard cheeses like Cheddar		skimmed milk, low fat or fat-free yoghurt, cottage cheese, curd cheese	
pork sausages, fatty meat, duck, goose	offal – heart, kidney, liver, brains, sweetbreads	lean meats – trim off fat, chicken, turkey	
	shellfish, fish roe	white fish like cod and plaice	fatty fish like herring and tuna
dripping, lard, hard margarine, coconut oil			corn oil, sunflower seed oil, safflower seed oil, cotton seed oil, polyunsaturated margarine

AVOID:		REPLACE WITH:	
Foods high in saturated fat and/or cholesterol	Foods high in cholesterol	Low fat/low cholesterol alternatives	Foods high in 'polyunsaturated fat' and low in cholesterol
egg yolk	egg yolk (limit to 2–3 per week)		
coconut, cashew nuts			most nuts
baked goods made with butter, margarine or egg yolks			baked goods made with corn oil and without egg yolks
chocolate, avocado			

Food	Cholesterol (mg/100g)	Cholesterol (mg/oz)
Dairy products		
Butter, salted	230	66
Cheese: Camembert	72	21
Cheddar	70	20
Cheese spread	71	20
Cottage cheese	13	4
Cream cheese	94	27
Danish blue	88	25
Edam	72	21
Parmesan	90	26
Processed cheese	88	25
Stilton	120	34
Cream, single	66	19
double	140	40
whipping	100	29
sterilized, canned	73	21
Milk, condensed, whole, sweetened	34	10
condensed, skimmed, sweetened	3	1
dried, whole	120	34
dried, skimmed	18	5
evaporated, whole, unsweetened	34	10
fresh whole	14	4
fresh, whole, Channel Islands	18	5
fresh, skimmed	2	Tr
longlife	14	4
sterilised	14	4
Yoghurt, low fat natural	7	2
flavoured	7	2
fruit	6	2
hazelnut	7	2

Food	Cholesterol (mg/100g)	Cholesterol (mg/oz)
Egg, whole, raw	450	129
white, raw	0	0
yolk, raw	1260	360
dried	1780	508
boiled	450	128
poached	480	137
omelette	410	117
scrambled	410	117
Egg and cheese dishes (home-made)		
Cauliflower cheese	17	5
Cheese soufflé	180	51
Macaroni cheese	20	6
Quiche Lorraine	130	37
Scotch egg	220	63
Welsh rarebit	67	19
Meat		
Bacon (raw, lean and fat)	57	16
(raw, lean only)	51	14
(fried, lean and fat)	80	23
(fried, lean only)	87	25
(grilled, lean and fat)	74	21
(grilled, lean only)	77	22
Beef (raw, lean and fat)	65	18
(raw, lean only)	59	17
(cooked, lean and fat)	82	23
(cooked, lean only)	82	23
Chicken (raw, light meat)	69	20
(raw, dark meat)	110	31
(boiled, light meat)	80	23
(boiled, dark meat)	110	31
(roast, light meat)	74	21

Food	Cholesterol (mg/100g)	Cholesterol (mg/oz)
Chicken, (roast, dark meat)	120	34
Duck (raw, meat only)	110	31
(roast, meat only)	160	46
Lamb (raw, lean and fat)	78	22
(raw, lean only)	79	22
(cooked, lean and fat)	110	31
(cooked, lean only)	110	31
Pork (raw, lean and fat)	72	21
(raw, lean only)	69	20
(cooked, lean and fat)	110	31
(cooked, lean only)	110	31
Rabbit (raw)	71	20
Turkey (raw, light meat)	49	14
(raw, dark meat)	81	23
(roast, light meat)	62	18
(roast, dark meat)	100	29
Meat products and dishes		
Beef, corned	85	24
Beefburgers (frozen, raw)	59	17
(frozen, fried)	68	19
Beefsteak pudding	30	8
Beef stew	30	8
Black pudding (fried)	68	19
Bolognese sauce	25	7
Brawn	52	15
Cornish pasty	49	14
Faggots	79	23
Frankfurters	46	13
Haggis (boiled)	91	26
Ham	33	10
Ham and pork, chopped	60	17

Food	Cholesterol (mg/100g)	Cholesterol (mg/oz)
Liver sausage	120	34
Luncheon meat	53	15
Polony	40	11
Pork pie, individual	52	15
Salami	79	23
Sausages, beef (raw)	40	11
beef (fried)	42	12
beef (grilled)	42	12
pork (raw)	47	13
pork (fried)	53	15
pork (grilled)	53	15
Sausage roll (flaky pastry)	20	6
(shortcrust pastry)	30	8
Saveloy	45	13
Shepherd's pie	25	7
Steak and kidney pie (pastry top)	125	36
Stewed steak with gravy	44	13
Veal, jellied	97	28
White pudding	22	6
Offal		
Brain, calf and lamb (raw)	2200	629
calf (boiled)	3100	886
lamb (boiled)	2200	629
Heart, lamb (raw)	140	40
sheep (roast)	260	74
ox (raw)	140	40
ox (stewed)	230	66
Kidney, Lamb (raw)	400	114
lamb (fried)	610	174
ox (raw)	400	114
ox (stewed)	690	197
pig (raw)	410	117

Food	Cholesterol (mg/100g)	Cholesterol (mg/oz)
Kidney, pig (stewed)	700	200
Liver, calf (raw)	370	106
calf (fried)	330	94
chicken (raw)	380	108
chicken (fried)	350	100
lamb (raw)	430	123
lamb (fried)	400	114
ox (raw)	270	77
ox (stewed)	240	69
pig (raw)	260	74
pig (stewed)	290	83
Oxtail (raw)	75	21
(stewed)	110	31
Sweetbread, lamb (raw)	260	74
(fried)	380	108
Tongue, lamb (raw)	180	51
sheep (stewed)	270	77
ox (boiled)	100	29
Tripe (dressed)	95	27
(stewed)	160	46
Fish and fish products		
Bloater (grilled)	80	23
Cod (fresh, raw)	50	14
(baked)	60	17
(grilled)	60	17
(poached)	60	17
(smoked, raw)	50	14
(smoked, poached)	60	17
(steamed)	60	17
Cockles	40	11
Crab (fresh)	100	29

Food	Cholesterol (mg/100g)	Cholesterol (mg/oz)
Crab (canned)	100	29
Fish fingers (frozen)	50	14
(fried)	50	14
Haddock (fresh, raw)	60	17
(fresh, steamed)	75	21
(smoked, steamed)	75	21
Halibut (raw)	50	14
(steamed)	60	17
Kipper (baked)	80	23
Lobster	150	43
Mackerel (raw)	80	23
(fried)	90	26
Mussels (raw)	100	29
Oysters (raw)	50	14
Plaice (raw)	70	20
(steamed)	90	26
Pilchards, canned in tomato sauce	70	20
Prawns	200	57
Roe, cod (hard, raw)	500	143
cod (hard, fried)	500	143
herring (soft, raw)	700	200
herring (soft, fried)	700	200
Saithe (raw)	60	17
(steamed)	75	21
Salmon (raw)	70	20
(canned)	90	26
(smoked)	70	20
(steamed)	80	23
Sardines, canned in oil, fish only	100	29
canned in tomato sauce	100	29
Scallops (raw)	40	11

Food	Cholesterol (mg/100g)	Cholesterol (mg/oz)
Scampi	110	31
Shrimps	200	57
Sole, lemon (raw)	60	17
(steamed)	60	17
Trout, steamed	80	23
Tuna, canned in oil	65	19
Whelks	100	29
Whiting (steamed)	110	31
Winkles	100	29
Fats and oils		
Butter, salted	230	66
Dripping, beef	60	17
Lard	70	20
Low fat spread	Tr	Tr
Margarine – cholesterol content will depend on the blend of oils used		
Suet, block	60	17
Suet, shredded	74	21
Vegetable oils	Tr	Tr
Baked goods and desserts		
Bread and butter pudding	100	29
Cheesecake	95	27
Christmas pudding	60	17
Custard, egg	100	29
Custard, made with powder	16	5
Custard tart	60	17
Dumpling	8	2
Eclairs	90	26
Fruit cake, rich	50	14
Gingerbread	60	17
Ice cream, dairy	21	6
non-dairy	11	3
Jelly, packet, cubes	0	0

Food	Cholesterol (mg/100g)	Cholesterol (mg/oz)
Jelly, made with water	0	0
made with milk	6	2
Lemon meringue pie	90	26
Meringues	0	0
Pancakes	65	19
Rock cakes	40	11
Sponge cake, with fat	130	37
without fat	260	74
Sponge pudding, steamed	80	23
Suet pudding, steamed	4	1
Trifle	50	14
Yorkshire pudding	70	20

The Good Health Guide £5.95

A splendidly illustrated encyclopaedia of the ways you and your family can enjoy healthy and satisfying lives, written by a team of Open University experts with the aim of linking your physical and psychological health to daily choices about the way you live.

'Comprehensive, attractive and lavishly illustrated. Fascinating and compelling . . . really excellent' YORKSHIRE POST

Dr Alan Maryon-Davis with Jane Thomas
Diet 2000 £1.75
how to eat for a healthier future

Diet 2000 is based on the latest medical research, recently published by the National Advisory Committee on Nutrition Education, which recommends new guidelines for healthier eating to combat the major diseases caused by the foods we eat today. Diet 2000 explains how easy it is to change your eating habits to achieve a balanced diet that is right for you. A revolutionary new guide to healthy eating for life.

Michael Wright
The Salt Counter £1

Too much salt in the diet is a major cause of many illnesses yet we eat on average twenty times our daily requirement. With excessive sodium in the diet being increasingly recognized as a significant health hazard, more and more health-conscious people are watching their salt intake. Here is an invaluable guide to how much salt you're eating in both natural and packaged foods, in every meal and snack.

Dr Andrew Stanway

Taking the Rough with the Smooth £1.95

The discovery that foods rich in dietary fibre (roughage) can help prevent the serious diseases of the affluent society has been heralded as the medical breakthrough of the decade. This is the definitive book on the subject written for the general reader.

Mouthwatering high-fibre recipes are included to enable readers to adapt their diets for a happier and healthier life.

Dr Richard Mackarness

Not All In The Mind £1.75

In this new vitally important book, Dr Richard Mackarness, doctor and psychiatrist, shows how millions may be made ill, physically and mentally, by common foods such as milk, eggs, coffee and white flour.

He relates case after case from his clinical practice where patients with chronic ailments resistant to other methods of treatment were cured by identifying and eliminating foods to which they had developed unsuspected allergy.

Chemical Victims £1.50

A startling new look at how chemicals in the environment are affecting your health. This book, by the bestselling author of *Not All in the Mind*, considers the long-term effects of the synthetic chemicals in our food and water, even in the air we breathe and whether more and more illness is being caused by man-made pollutants. There are no comfortable answers. Dr Mackarness – widely experienced in clinical research into food and chemical allergies – suggests that 'problem' patients are not being helped by more and more surgery and drugs; careful avoidance of the chemicals that cause migraine, depression, fatigue, skin and bowel disorders could be the cure.

Mary Laver and Margaret Smith

Diet for Life £2.50

a cookbook for arthritics

Written by an arthritic for sufferers everywhere, this cookbook explains the principles of a dietary regime that offers new hope of a normal active life free from the crippling pain of arthritis. A step-by-step guide to almost two hundred recipes, avoiding animal fats and fruit and using the minimum of additives; varied and interesting eating to take full advantage of the range of fresh vegetables as they come into season.

D. C. Jarvis, MD

Folk Medicine £1.95

The tough, hard-living mountain folk of the state of Vermont have a time-honoured folk medicine.

The late Dr Jarvis, a fifth generation native of Vermont, lived and practised among these sturdy people for over fifty years. This book is the result of his deep study of their way of life and in particular of their concepts of diet. These he was able to test against his formal medical training and prove by long experience.

He offers a new theory on the treatment and prevention of a wide variety of ailments – the common cold, hay fever, arthritis, high blood pressure, chronic fatigue, overweight and many others – and holds out a promise of zestful good health for young and old.

Arthritis & Folk Medicine £1.75

When folk medicine swept through Britain and America with its amazing message of relief from countless diseases, the author received innumerable letters from sufferers from arthritis, lumbago, gout and muscular rheumatism, enquiring what folk medicine had to offer them for their misery.

Now Dr Jarvis replies – explaining step by step a simple, sensible method of treatment, evolved through generations of trial and error by the rugged folk of his native Vermont and meticulously tested against his own medical experience.

Malcolm Jayson and Allan Dixon
Rheumatism and Arthritis £2.50

This excellent, readable and highly informative book covers every aspect of rheumatic and arthritic conditions, and offers a survey of the very latest techniques of treatment. It examines recent developments in this area of research where hundreds of millions of pounds are spent annually, and the possibilities of the breakthrough thousands are waiting for. Dispelling the medical mystique that disturbs so many patients, here is well-informed, common-sense advice for sufferers from one of the most common diseases.

'One copy of this book is worth at least ten copper bracelets'
NEW SCIENTIST

Barbara Griggs
The Home Herbal £1.95

As more and more people turn to alternative medicines and therapies, here is an authoritative and practical guide to herbal remedies, what they are, where to get them and how to use them. The book is organized alphabetically under the medical problems – for which conventional medicine can often fail or produce unpleasant side-effects, or in those minor cases where natural, gentle treatment is preferable – and herbal remedies are suggested under each of these headings – from acne to whooping cough. Additional chapters describe the preparation of herbal medicines, where to find herbs, and common and botanical names.

general editor Miriam Stoppard
The Face and Body Book £5.95

The practical guide to looking good, based firmly on the principle that beauty is an accessible reality for women of all ages. Miriam Stoppard's team of no-nonsense experts give practical illustrated advice on every aspect of good looks, providing insight and inspiration for every woman who wants to enjoy the best of good looks, health and fitness. Sections include face and body, make-up, diet and nutrition, exercise, relaxation, sleep, beauty treatments, alternative medicine.

Irwin Maxwell Stillman, MD and Samm Sinclair Baker

The Doctor's Quick Weight Loss Diet £1.50

Vital truths about effective dieting. Over sixty quick reducing diets to fit every problem and taste . . . This book contains no way-out theories or strange concoctions. Its instructions are simple to understand, easy to follow – and have proved dramatically effective by the eminent and experienced doctor who wrote this highly-acclaimed work.

Coach Jim Everroad

How to Flatten Your Stomach £1.50

An exercise programme devised by an expert. It takes only a few minutes each day. It's so easy that anyone can do it and it really does work!

Coach Jim Everroad and Lonna Mosow

How to Trim Your Hips and Shape Your Thighs £1.50

From the author of *How to Flatten Your Stomach*. Devised by the experts, a new figure and fitness exercise programme that really does work!